Freedom Light
Expressions of Hope and Evidence

Poetry

Glen Aubrey

www.Freedom-Light.com
www.CreativeTeamPublishing.com

Creative Team Publishing

Creative Team Publishing
San Diego

© 2009 by Glen Aubrey
All rights reserved. No part of this book may be reproduced, stored in a retrieval system, or transmitted in any form or by any means without the prior written permission of the publisher, except by a reviewer who may quote brief passages in a review to be printed in a newspaper, magazine, or journal.

First Printing

ISBN: 978-0-9797358-7-5
PUBLISHED BY CREATIVE TEAM PUBLISHING
www.CreativeTeamPublishing.com
San Diego

Printed in the United States of America

Freedom Light
Expressions of Hope and Evidence

Poetry

Glen Aubrey

www.Freedom-Light.com
www.CreativeTeamPublishing.com

It is not okay, in fact, it's wrong to allow another's experiences, opinions, and beliefs to frame yours when you possess powerful, God-given, unique opportunities and capabilities to explore and learn for yourself.

Your quests for enduring, principled truth and life application should include acquiring information from proven instructors whom you respect but must not be limited exclusively to their proclamations or interpretations. Apart from personal exploration—your own discovery, struggle, and conclusions—your journey is not complete.

Dedication

Sincerity is a choice of positive attitude and devotion at profound depths of reason, spirit, and emotion. It is a trait shared by balanced and maturing people, those not content with cursory, unproven, ritualistic simplicities. Sincerity pierces walls of insecurity, dissuades dogmatic inhibitions, and reveals and removes unnerving distractions. You are exercising sincerity when you engage fully in quests to enrich your life and the lives of others.

Freedom Light is dedicated to people of sincerity. If you are a searcher unsatisfied with anything other than continuing processes of dedicated discovery, accept that you are numbered with a few consecrated souls. These people of integrity and inward determination recognize that one of God's greatest gifts is desire, the insatiable longing for knowledge, faith, maturity, activity, and enduring right relationships.

If you, like me, are one who yearns for more, read on. This work is for us.

Table of Contents

Preface 13

Poetry 17

A Choice Away 19
A Long Road Home 21
A Promise 23
Adjustments 25
Adventures 27
Alterations 29
Attraction 31
Beneath 33
Between 35
Cadence 37
Certain Sights and Sounds 39
Close 41
Closure 43
Cold 45
Comfort 47
Companionship 49
Considerations 51
Cornerstones 53
Created to Fly 55
Crossings 57
Definition 59
Demands 61
Demise 63
Departures 65
Disappointment 67

Division 69
Does God Change His Mind? 71
Dogma 73
Enclosures 77
End 79
Endurance 81
Environment 83
Episode 85
Exceptions to the Rules 87
Expectation 89
Finality 91
Foundations 93
Freedom's Recompense 95
Fulfillment 97
Gentle Rain 99
Grains of Sand Alone 101
Gratitude 103
Illumination 105
Immortalized 107
In the Eyes of a Child 109
In the Silence 111
Inspiration 113
Interest 115
Keep the Dream Alive (poem) 117
Keep the Dream Alive (music) 119
Labels 121
Learned Once More 123
Learning 125
Lengthening Shadows 127
Linger 129
Live to Last 131
Lonesome Grace 133
Longing 135
Loss 137
Memory's Chords 139

Monuments 141
More than Hope 143
Morning Comes 145
Music 147
Music is Stirring 149
Nearly Persuaded 151
No Words 153
Now 155
Occupying Space, Spending Time 157
Opportunity 159
Passing on the Bridge 161
Persuasion, Permission, Perspective 163
Profound Expressions 165
Quiet Contemplation 167
Rescue 169
Restful Recompense 171
Return 173
Rocking Chairs and Scented Candles 175
Scenes 177
Seeking for More 179
Snow 181
Softer 183
Solemnity 185
Somehow 187
Sovereign 189
Spoken 191
Star Struck 193
Sure Rewards 195
The Blank Page 197
The Chorused Freedom 199
The Old Piano 201
The Passion 203
The Return 205
They Cannot Speak 207
This Time 209

Time 211
Unclouded Eyes 213
Welcomed Home 215
Well Done 217
Were It Not So Different 219
When What Is Dreamt 221
When, Where, Why, How 223

Afterword 225

Acknowledgements 229

The Author 231

The Publisher 233

Products 235

Preface

A sequel to *Go From the Night*, this collection of poetry, *Freedom Light—Expressions of Hope and Evidence* occupies its place in support of profound expressions of human struggle, quests for truth, longings of the heart, and enduring answers born of confident assurance. While both books are independent creations, they express expanded meaning through each other.

Upon what do your beliefs rest? Of what are you sure? Confidence resides in a cooperative relationship of two essential components. These elements are *hope* and *evidence*. These terms are important. Let's define them.

From *Core Teams Work Their Principles and Practices*, page 96: "Hope is a wish or a dream, but it is also more. Here it constitutes a strong and continuing desire for the good, right, and true. Hope that does not disappoint, and is not disappointed, focuses and frames best results that may come to pass if enough diligent effort is put forth.

"The second element is evidence. This is proof of a result that is sure to come. When right motives and dedicated actions are combined toward fulfillment of a worthwhile endeavor, evidence states that winning will occur. Completion of a goal may reside in the future, but the indication of good outcome is based on confirmed and irrefutable testimony. History proves that enduring and positive results come to pass when correct belief and right action are purposefully aligned and combined."*

Freedom Light presents poetic expressions of hope and evidence. Its purpose is to build faith and faithfulness where confidence is embraced and applied freely, overcoming doubt while supporting endless journeys of inquiry.

A venture apart from enlightenment and encouragement can be

immeasurably long and ultimately unfulfilled, certainly unfruitful. This book encourages you to live in confidence, and to experience internal satisfaction, assured of outcomes because you live in truth.

Freedom Light explores release from distraction, and provides motivation to creatively act and respond. Life lessons born of truth and borne on duplicative examples are validated through the ages, beyond time. They reside in principles and verifiable actions where positive results flourish and from which great stories are composed and told. This book celebrates their composition and contributions to a person's well being.

Approach the stanzas with openness, inquisitiveness, certainty, and resilient dedication. Transcend any initial lack of understanding or a void of immediate gratification. Poetry, often by intent, is designed to stimulate the reader to express him or herself within life-tried teaching where interpretations are sought, surrendered, and sanctioned.

Your quests are important. Impacted by needs of the moment while anchored to ideals of the past, integrity-driven investigations live within the frameworks of eternally abiding truth.

Your perspectives differ from those of others. Bring yours with you, employ them, never cease to ask questions, try to define what you discover, and wonder at what you cannot see materially.

Your life will be richer for the adventure as will the experiences of those who, like you search steadily for ultimate realizations, many of which may not be fulfilled in this life. Seek them regardless.

As you read, appreciate your options, your golden opportunities. Enjoy every minute of discovery. Every one counts for more than anyone could possibly envision.

Let's begin.

* Please see the following websites for business, leadership, and team development books by Glen Aubrey:
  www.LeadershipIs.com
  www.IndustrialStrengthSolutions.com
  www.CoreTeamsWork.com
  www.Lead52.com
  www.Lincoln-Leadership-Gettysburg.com

Poetry

A Choice Away

Nearly removed,
Viewed from afar ere longing dies,
Desire churns from secreted innermost regions, seeking to be
    replenished.

Nourished, a pilgrim recognizes distraught yet familiar voices
Piercing love's lost and latent, distanced voids
Where destinies abide subjected to their owners.

Cloistered, moved upon the board,
Represented, yet unreachable,
Restless hearts seek reasons and reach for the unattainable.

Choices beam a dream's pursuit in graceful diligence
Where remains the perfect plan,
Though oft its stains and scars are permanent.

A Long Road Home

Roaming,
Wandering purposelessly
Through fog-shrouded lanes
Where precise distance, difficult to measure
Moves perspectives toward narrowed sights,
Raise cautions,
Heighten sensitivities,
Stimulate latent senses,
Open minds.

Loneliness dissolves, discontented.
Believe there must be sufficient warmth
To evaporate long-graying, gradient's foreboding mists.

Determination restores deserted souls.
Removed, walls, tunneled pasts, fade
Though coarse goads remain and restrain.

Shining radiance dissuades distraught memories,
Dispersing, dissipating them.
Refreshment's smiling rebirth
Lifts fogs
As do comforting spirits' gentler songs
Whose homeward journeys
Seize the prizes as rewards of submission and salvation.
Cradle its promises, hold noninvasive friendships closer,
Refresh a precious, uplifted heart.

A Promise

The one unfulfilled may be the one never uttered, rather, assumed,
    Or, proclaimed, evinced through futile longings,
        Undefined, unrealized, discarded potentials
    Declared and focused upon emotions' motions solely,
        Worked, massaged, and inappropriately influencing desired effects.

Manipulation is a child of greed.

Placating none, higher inspiration requires and molds spaces for authentic inquisitors.
    Doubters may believe and remain in the clan.
        They are parts of the plan, too.
    Who shall openly greet, confront, and respond to genuine desires for truth?
        Obedience's commands demand a promise spoken, heard, honored, and fulfilled.

Adjustments

Identifying and dealing with obvious distractions—
Toils not easily done.
They are necessary, though.

Nuisances won't wait.
Cloaked in pervasive interruptions they must be dealt with.

Bothersome people and their deeds
Require carefully weighed options of approach.

Adjust yourself before attempting to repair others.
It works.

See them through the eyes of personal responsibility.
Necessarilyfillvacatedrelationshipsbeyondsurfaceexpectation.
Realignments move to conclude redemption's cause.

Adventures

Events, driving, riding aloft torrential change
For a time
Force objects once believed immovable, to shift.
These are nourished by The Inevitable.

Greed grins when appearances declare a win and its loss.
Through truism emerges the blessed champion,
Dancing away the past, piercing its now, consecrating a future's terms,
Rising improved for the tempests and storms, restored, strengthened, and resilient beyond measure.

Breast milk feeds innocence.
Dependent little ones possess and control no alternative options.
Love takes over and it should.
Experiences charm all manner of attendees.

Gatherings nurture a communion of likes.
Whispering winds, chorusing frogs, murmuring streams, cawing crows, wispy clouds, hidden moons,
Misty celestials, daylight's delicacies, candle-flickering escapes, repeating rhythms, foreboding shadows, chills, and spills
Speak volumes, though none may be interpreted fully.

Divergent gazes, beckoning eyes, longings gleaned from
    alternative perspectives
Cease to divide the Truly Interested.
Drawn to union,
Oneness guarantees more to the few and less to the many.

Lingering longings demand solemnity at depths nearly
    unreachable,
Eradicatingnotdesperateneedsforcontemplativeisolation'swalls
Where creativities, bold in their environments,
Contribute wares though often through toil and struggle.

A second glass,
Another's pass,
Age weighs heavily upon the bearer
Who must achieve a greater good while time and opportunity
    remain.

Alterations

Altered views, transformed directions,
Life's longed-for preparations
Temporarily suspended,
An animation's anticipation.

Dramatic differences, distinct characteristics,
Morphed enough, become desires.
Images fade beneath unfiltered lights,
Searching truism's staying power.

Freely adjusted behaviors originate not from contrived,
    controlled, and coerced experiences,
Altar-laden, emotion-driven, compliance-counted,
Found wanting.
Yanked, pulled adrift, anchors let go.

Abide.
Ride winds and waves whose encumbrances become natural,
    universal elements applied inexorably.
Chart beneficial courses aright.
Ruins, rocks, and roles accompany change.

Attraction

Radiant, inward beauty relies not at all on cursory trappings of tired and worn-out replicas.
Reach beneath and reveal a primary makeup unaffected by trendy, temporary façades.

It doesn't take much time to discover what is not.
It does, however, take a lifetime to value and uphold what is.

Motives play, authoring diverse techniques of effective communication.
Meaningful responses weigh a sincere questioner's intents.

Self proclamation is a loss developing.
Mindful recognition, benefiting another, is the most attractive of all.

Beneath

Underlined, underscored foundations,
Formed of more than fortune's wishes,
Remain immovable when tried.

Veterans' epitaphs
Fair to behold mid rows of markers
Etch service, birth, conflict, death.

War consumes
While causes for which conflicts rage
Push victorious and enduring ones to pause and reflect.

Beneficiaries comprehend mere fragments of the magnitude of sacrifice,
Accept monumental relinquishments of the dearest of gifts on altars of belief
Where ideas born of idealism are fixed upon stone forever.

Between

Fixed yet fluid,
Determined yet delicate,
Final yet finite,
Blessings reverberate though dragged over rough hewn places.

Some term them rewards,
Others, rest.
All enjoy their refreshments,
Few relish their test.

Learning transpires, regardless.
Reception's guarantee looms not larger
In solemn sublimity
But, awestruck, one wonders what the future holds

For which preparations amid throws
Mold opportunity,
Build endurance,
Increase strengths.

Cadence

A cadence, offered up freely, ascending descending scales, in
 opposition performed,
Presents contrasting, completing harmonies,
Melodious,
Mastered pieces.
Attractive antitheses
Invite, repel, tugging at the senses, demanding worship.
Torn but not confused, informed hearers,
Interpretive listeners,
Understand structure, even intent.
Elevated beyond comprehension,
They marvel as enchanted emotions pierce staid barricades.
Revel once more at unexplainable ecstasies
Wrought within an art form's executed, exalted magnificence.
Rapture at these levels few even realize exists.
Imagined, perceived, or experienced as knowledge merely,
Even fewer dwell within intimacy's enduring embrace,
A sacred domain where fullness, exhortative,
Amazing, and reverential,
Sets wonders apart in praise and adoration.

Certain Sights and Sounds

Aromas cause it, too—a longing soul's reminders of priceless
    treasures
Long buried, hidden, dormant—
Rediscovered when stimuli invade the ordinary by surprise.

Negative recollections,
Awash in defeatism,
Rise to be noticed, mixing with the good.

Art emerges, shoves debris aside, uplifts the downtrodden.
Feelings glisten, memory bows, giving place to gratitude.
Certainties usher unadulterated joy into the recesses of the soul.

Close

Nearby, nearly touching,
Attuned to fleeting breaths, sensing softer movements,
Thrilling to cooperative and competing cravings,
Reeling from the shared and sheer rustling of winds,
Two, in solitude, pass by,
Each oblivious to all
Save the proximity of the other.

Personas hidden,
Sight lines occluded, forbidden
As though they had never met,
Or linked associations, yet
Running brooks' flows
Still mount desires to bury their falls
While nature blooms, season to season.

Parallel finds,
Different kinds
Positioned, their minds
Purposefully reflect on beautiful days
Gone,
Marking separate ways,
Ne'er to be returned.

O'er shallow's streams
Shadow's walkways'
Fallowed grounds
May bear
Sequential alternatives.
May these close
By one more, be?

Mid intangible perceptions,
Grasping, releasing profuse effects,
Creating soul mates
Out of distinct and distant persons
Who otherwise
Would have remained apart,
Disparate proximity diminishes when compared to timed and
    treasured tenderness.

Closure

Proofs, tags of decisive conclusion impossible to remove
Arrest a sharpened mind, sensitize a broken heart, rejuvenate
    a restless spirit, and revive a neglected soul.
Binding tie's effects are strong.

Memories linger,
Longings lost punctuate recurring reflections,
Those of what was then that shall not be lived again.

Overwhelmingprivationsoftemitadvancewarningsoftheircoming,
These should not be ignored or refused;
Rather, recognized, respected, and acted upon.

Living in fear is foreign to ones who are prepared.
Widened understandings watch for the uncommon.
Beneath surfaces of the ordinary they pitch intents.

Finality comes although difficult to embrace.
Sorrow-filled, regret-enhanced, timed to needs of maturing
    individuals,
Foreordained or spontaneous, it appears.

Closure is not exclusively an end.
It is the very process of reaching its points.
Acceptance welcomes emotions, predicted, surprising,
    unnerving, or exhilarating.

Add significance.
Values live beyond and in spite of pain.
Turn the latch, open inviting though imposing doors of discovery;
    these adventures carry wonderers on.

Cold

Piercing and defensive, boring through the outermost thickened layers,
Biting the bones,
Defying the strongest admonitions,
Retold on stones,

Bitterness reigns, gripping the soul.
Meaningless conversations, dreary silence, permanently infused negativity,
Inflame throngs moaning their insufficiencies,
Succumbing to calls for demise.

Deserted smiles cheer no one.
Embrace's warmth erases naught.
Against an enemy's tightened knot
Converted ones expire.

Does it have so to be?
Destined with singular ability,
Can bonds be broken, warmth restored,
Gracefulness reestablished, welcoming sustainable and profitable futures?

In a word, yes.

Comfort

Coming from closest, foreordained, or least expected sources,
Graciously carried and gratefully received,
Assuagement of the heart is welcomed from the depths of the soul.
Comfort one another.

Some refuse these overtures, appearing content.
Lost, isolation blinds them in insecurity.
Others misuse the gift, substituting façades for truth,
Manipulating, posturing, selfishly recompense-driven.

Consolatory expressions emerge from the comforted.
Their favors are authentic,
Warmly enfolding all
Who give and receive them humbly.

Companionship

Utterances, heard or imagined within states of being
Where sweet communion with those who lovingly,
Willingly participate in cooperative engagements,

Apart from the required,
Align in soulfully rearranged combinations,
Hearkening to hopes and dreams of the beloved.

Where a quest's importance exceeds its tests
Fears disappear in flows' assurances, displacing struggles'
    fruitlessness.
Smiling warmth is but one keepsake.

Strengths balance timidity with resolve,
Mellow the forced, and encourage the downtrodden.
Joy comes to longing and fulfilling hearts.

Considerations

Length
      Breadth
Pulse
      Breath
Height
      Depth
Life
      Death

Considerations, all.

Creatures grasp to learn, believe.
From this quest reigns no reprieve.

Close to one,
Another's lost.
Yours the mission,
Yours the cost.

Stay
      Go
Fast
      Slow
Fore
      Go
Their
      "No."

Cornerstones

Accusatory, emptied voices
Proclaim nothing of permanent importance.
They rely on immaterial, insufficient, wrongful conceptions.
Their inconclusiveness rules merely o'er engrossed
discomfiture's dregs.

Tapped out,
Trapped in excessive, warped requirements,
Fulfillment's goal
Yields to nemesis's greed, control.

Changing image, wrapping toads,
Stifled essence, screaming goads
Crave allegiance wrongly sought,
From distressed, disturbed, distraught.

Cornerstones, laid sure to dwell,
Outlast storms, enduring hell.
Battled, tried, endurance reigns.
Blessed, these efforts win their gains.

Created to Fly

Sheltered, secured, warm, at home,
The daughter, first born, rests, matures,
She awaits her time.
A child of God, she is a gift of love.

Her name means "Little Bird."
She will fly, she will soar.
Like her namesake
She may rescue the leader of a nation.

Her father will provide,
Her mother will protect,
Her family will adore,
Her friends will follow her.

One day she will take the wings of the dawn.
Our world soon shall receive the gifts
Of tenderness and truth her coming offers.
"Life," may you reign in graceful beauty, loved and little one.

Written in 2009 in honor of Zipporah, "Zoey," my granddaughter.

Crossings

Permanently fixed, unknown,
Advancing reality
Questions surrounding presences.
It craves the answers of who, when, where, and why.

Against unequaled despair concerning ill will, pointed inward,
Exceeding players and their capability's senses,
Reason directs, molding ends
Born of chance and chosen parts.

There's no going back,
Theirs are not returned.
Surfaced appearances,
Odds cooperate freely

When observed from distanced views.
Before, afterwards,
Decision's complexities
Remain swept and sweeping.

Definition

Ways, means, forms, and substance
Require explanation if understanding is to be achieved.

Challenges, opportunities, and rewards
Present contributions revealed in the definitions they become.

Clarity determines focus, allegiance a comprehensive dedication.
Fulfill a dream whose cause is greater than its attending
    circumstances.

Life is too short to allow obscurity's confusion where, aimlessly
    wandering,
One's person and purpose are lost in ambiguity.

Which provide definitions for your supreme endeavors?
    Laws
            Graces
                  People
                          Places
  Peers
          Seers
                History
                        Fears
    Victories
           Tears
                 Vacuums
                        Sneers

Reliable definitions
Reside within tried and tested frameworks.

Clarity may constitute an initial, valued payment.
Closure follows upon actions born of understanding and
    agreement.

Unveil pathways in front of your feet.
Knowledge is abandoned where first steps remain untried.

Demands

Allegiance bought is seldom sought for reasons beyond
    self-gratification.
Demagoguery thrives on forging chains, fencing in free spirits
Who, roaming free, create and dwell within miraculous worlds of
    wonder.
Embracing and exceeding expectations, reaching depths and
    heights heretofore unrevealed,
These hearty souls do not thrive within the mediocre standards
    of any environment.

Insecurities imbibe deficiency's demands to frame a construct's
    prison walls
Wherein dwell the dreamless, damaged, and destitute
Who await no consummation, disintegrating, alone.
Divested of station yet destined within it, they endure self-
    wrought chains remorsefully.
Regrets emerge mid tumultuous, confusing thoughts.

Consider societal evolution's rigid religiosity
As mundane and momentary,
Satisfying little if any true beats of the ingenuous heart
While uplifted themes, purer songs await departing throngs
Rising beyond and before what they ever dreamt was possible.

Demise

It comes to us all.

An artisan's epitaph,
A tombstone's etched remembrances,
Reveal not enough.
Curious, those who glance briefly, forget.

Instructions crafted in stone,
Remain.
Recordings are repositories.
Libraries exceed memory.

Quests wrench hungry ones away.
Demise opens unfamiliar but required doors.
Those unsatisfied with surface explorations
Walk through these opportune passages with unwavering
    determination.

Experience the beyond.
Fear or faith restrain no one.

Departures

Familiar, family-tied or friendship-bound,
Legacy emerges from an accumulation of experiences.
Who receives these time-sensitized eternal offerings?
Other worldly, foreign, unusual models encourage gifting
    without reservation.

Testimonials, spoken, lived, thrive, multiply, infectious in healthy ways
While learned lessons are taught anew in contemporary tales.
Olden truths, current applications—
These never expire though departures come and go.

Fondly held, pleasant recollections mist the eyes.
A remnant remains, silent, unexpressed in public forums.
Memories prepare discomforting passages.
Passersby know not, some attendees care not.

For those who grasp empirical and eternal truth in cooperation
The ever-present, what matters most, relates truth
    experientially.
Received, sifted, tested, and proven by caring ones,
Sincere, secure, maturing people, listening, contribute to greatness.

Disappointment

Little changes.
Disaffected results from faulty endeavors
Produce nothing substantive.
Disappointments weary those who fruitlessly try to alter natural outcomes.

Leaning, sacrificing one's own stamina
Bodes ill
For no one understands who does not stand alone
When final tallies are collected and disbursed.

Hope reigns in you
And others proven worthy,
Receiving, giving allegiance,
Time-tested, shown to be real.

Though careworn, value viability
Ere disappointment lingers beyond a reasonable expectation.
Personal paths of achievement fashion motive and momentum.
Create and pursue diligently what you know to be true.

Division

Universal, peaceful coexistence is impossible
Apart from compromise that must of necessity
Uproot fundamentally held beliefs of groups in opposition.

It is, therefore, unachievable minus conflict.
One wins,
Another loses.

If all bow, who leads, who follows?
The ones to whom deference is paid command willful or coerced
    allegiance.
Obedience shuns dissent.

        Division remains.

Conflict, mid enlightened understandings and overtures of
    peace, momentarily restrained, emerges anew in altered forms
    if the basis points of one side are not changed.
Conquests pit ideologies, contrary systems, against each other.
Protectionism and arrogance thrive within perspectives their
    owners are convinced are true.

God cannot be for and against
Opposing opinions and cross-purposed practices all at the same time.
Willing agreements do not exist where one party's win is another's loss.
Forced compliance is the mandate and mission of those who conquer.

Does God Change His Mind?

Understanding etherial works of faith,
  Influenced mightily from momentary expediency,
    Can it be concluded that simply what feels good reveals
      God's blessing or His curse?

How is omniscient will demonstrated thus?
  How could we ever know for sure?
  Will we?

Does God Change His Mind?
  Do circumstances alter His foreordained plans?
  What of those originating from other-earthly experiences
    that participants are convinced are true?

When one is sure of what is right, secure in perceptions of
  righteous courses,
    Should not circumstances, regardless of sources, be
      weighed against objective reality?
    The proof of a claim, where endurance toward completion
      is not deemed optional, proves commitment no matter
      degrees of difficulty or ease of fulfillment.

Is a claim used merely to satisfy one's perception of truth?
  Shall shallowness be accepted when challenges come?
  Should escapes reveal alternatives, dissuading the surface-
    borne believer?

Does God Change His Mind
    Or are human viewpoints easily changed?
    What of yours?

Dogma

Struggling, strained, multi-layered, filtered philosophies, argumentative,
Concentrating immense energies on mediocre, surfaced non-essentials,
Refusing then denying creative contributions' perspectives,
Wastelands where interpretations exist merely in throws of shallow, controvertible biases,

Cult-like, designed to be imposed upon dimmed but willing minds, those of unsuspecting, ignorant masses,
When given the right impetus and opportunity,
Invade with impudence, often without warning, dispelling and disbursing their opinions o'er wide expanses
As dulled audiences hypnotically succumb to fear-entrenched, dogma-driven, improbable, and unproven theories.

Freed thinkers, unshackled though engulfed by simplicity's so-called sacred and sacrificial offerings
Allow places to remain for sonorous, smile-masked, faked, and arrogant voices
Whose worth captured in tallied and toilsome tones,
Still sways lost and uninitiated ones.

Only within deluded minds
Are fleeting, self-aggrandizing performers
Able to lure blindly submissive, sleepy audiences.
Flattery, in the end, benefits bearers alone.

Informed intelligence seeks loftier keeps, broadened views,
    sacred rites, legacy-infused.
Grounded, perennially unquenched desires remain for immortal
    nourishment.
These sustain age-tried, experience-borne, immovable, and
    undeniable truths.
Inquisitive, secure sojourners crave deeper meaning unceasingly,
    searching reality until death prevents further quests.

Dogma's imposters impartially control minds, missions, means.
Ends unclear, rehearsed, defined in dated terminology,
    pragmatically void,
Relinquish character for a latest fad's recompense.
Domination replaces genuine desires, those born of gratified,
    satisfied, and giving hearts.

Power becomes its self-served goal, greed-driven, unquenchable,
Addressing massed individuals' needs in images only,
Where primary, if not soulful purposes try to satiate the authors'
    insecurities even as their base is intentionally led astray.
These leaders disparage dependability and dwell in deception.

Followers, blinded or comforted within woefully entrapping
    ignorance, wander as in a stupor and even support the
    dysfunctional enterprise.
These neither count nor amount to too much beyond their
    graves; they are good only while they live, targets of greed,
Saved not, nor uplifted in the company of inheritance-blessed
    children of a greater promise
Who respectfully cherish then birth full-spectrum life-views as
    they become revealed.

Denied, refused temporarily and oft without cause beyond the
    immediate self-gratification of evil bent,
Power-hungry mongers, those who disagree with well-meaning,
    honest discovery,
Cite inconsequential, fear-burdened, contextually misplaced,
    intentional, mono-perspective-graced non-essentials and
    bold-faced lies
Until revealed treasures, long-sought, unearthed, are weighed
    and willingly purchased.

Dogmas are crushed beneath the bare feet of pilgrims newly
    freed, or ground into dust from the ill-fitting clogs worn by
    those who have long traveled these ancient paths.
All must trod here shorn of shoes or wearing them, whether
    they fit or not.
Liberated, those who think, believe, and compose fresh ideas
Duplicate lasting conclusions and wash the feet of the weary
    traveler.

Scenes anew,
Birthed from old,
Learned, teach truths
Pure as gold.

Enclosures

Traps? No, nor escapes;
Rather, secured frames wherein perspectives—
Independent, blended, opaque, clear, nondescript, definitive—
Dictate needs for clarification and compromise.

Looking outward from an inward soul's earnest desires,
Piercing excuses of a closed environment's confines,
Longings for truth break the bonds of immature comprehension,
And design places where liberated imagination reigns.

Searcher's leanings deliver balanced views of strength.
These redefine nomenclature,
Conquer perception's walls of doubt,
Merge vistas, dissolve mists, and watch as pitched variances dim.

Enclosures? No, nor cages;
Rather, structures whose architectural drawings—
Portraying intents—
Rarely conform to extremity-laden, emboldened strictures,
    strongholds sure.

You are invited to stay and expand the courses that shape and
    share your destiny.

End

The song's conclusion dwells not in its refrain, nor within
    its coda.
Repetition's purpose abruptly ceases when a phrase is
    repeated too often.
Closure disrupts a growing potential or finishes its sentence.
There are no other options here.

Until then, decide the worth of endeavor.
Engender contributions formed to exceed and excel
Planned anticipation's immediate application and gratification.
These opportunities exist, and you must find them.

Known mediums, touching reality's senses,
Ask, "What realms outside experience truly can be measured?"
Answers over time only do their stories tell.
Passages find, define, and transverse their Fine while secrets remain,
    destined so.

All the more reason to fully embrace and enjoy rapturing moments
Within frameworks of enduring truth.
Finally, a perspective with which all agree to some degree:
An ending comes, like it or not.

Endurance

Tough it out—exercise endurance beyond discouragement and
    disappointment—
Do what you must.
Laws of ages past discard reinterpretations.
Refuse to bundle messes or to join their bungling masses.
Rise above surface-bound incongruities.
Chart personal destiny principle-driven, inspiration-formed.
Play what you possess.
Discover what you need.

Because you will, make it so.
Alive, remember you are not alone, nor shall you ever be.
Supported, loved, your innermost regions' needs speak, and
    universal truths respond.
Fill your vessels, occupy vacuums, focus directives, accomplish
    goals.
Allow self-evidence to emerge and develop differently than
    anyone may have imagined.
Desires formed of distant dreams will be brought closer as
    abilities embrace life-change.
Seek, create, and accept alterations for what they are, and for
    what they must come.
Revelatory, life will germinate its own, determining its destiny.

Environment

Embedded, intertwined throughout coarse atmospheres,
Longings for respite mature as life-altering instructions pervade,
Moving souls of saint and sinner
To weigh alternatives of superior choices, then decide.

Values, essential principles, respond to any challenge,
Define importance, and empower activity.
Pauses refresh opportunities for development within reality's frame.
Knowledge, in wisdom, presents itself to eager inquirers.

What must one do?
Considerations originate from listening to, sifting through, and evaluating interrogatories.
Compare present motives and means with purer and lovelier ones.
Desired outcomes may request a change to your surroundings.

Episode

Turnings of tides, realignments regenerated,
Forces exceeding comprehension or refusal
Close one epoch, open another.

Deeming timed periods,
Episodes may diminish initial impact.
They must be seen for what they compose and what they don't.

Remembrances are rejuvenated by personal world views.
Commonalities take revitalized forms
While rotations of seasons, circumstances, relationships, and
    treasures, come.

Collected versions beg for esteem or at least a hearing.
Granting recognition assigns value, validates perspective,
Evaluates longevity, and proclaims the blessed worth of core
    essence.

History's retelling alters no facts,
Only how they are viewed and felt.
Events remain for what they are and all they have become.

Significantly affecting acquaintances, appearances abound
    within perceived congeniality.
Greater longings willfully risk rudeness, interjecting purposeful
    questions
Toward determined understanding of an era's meaning.

Sources of answers frame comprehension and intentionally
    shape outcomes.
The positions and parts you play belong to you, alone.
Welcome a sojourner who desires to perform opposite your
    antics.

Exceptions to the Rules

Anomalies, so called, are more common than most would care to
    admit.
        They burst on the scene,
        Invited or not.

What are the origins of ruling rigidity?
        Like pencils with too-soft sharpened lead,
        They soon break under pressures born of necessity.

Strains and pains subsist in corners of minds and events.
        These, if counted as equals,
        Suffer to be sheltered by the more enduring ones.

They effect far less than their reputations propose.
        Yet, afforded undue attention,
        They shine with more brilliance than the brightest stars.

They fool the inflexible,
        Confound the careful,
        Discombobulate the cautious,

        They wonder at grasped victories too easily won.

What frames your exceptions?
    Whence are formed your rules?
        When emerges grander destiny?
            Who are greater fools?

Expectation

A hard word, this.

Its renderings
    Pervade personhood and rival responsibility.

Two, the realistic and the un-
    Command complex reflection if any should be won.

What or who
    Defines what lasts?

Controlling assignors of duties asked
    Force compliance to rules and tasks.

These matter too much, too often.
    Impact cannot be avoided when unearthed character shines forth.

Wise are the receptors
    Who weigh an expectation against measured realism.

Finality

It isn't discovered in striving nor does it come in this life.

Efforts expended toward securing futures
Bear their results when death takes charge.

They always do.

No matter.
Initiatives continue to preserve what should be treasured
When the veil is crossed.

Diligent designs, in appearance well-intentioned,
Flail and fume when life diminishes and families take over.
Unmitigated greed accompanies attempts at resolution.

Submission to whims and wants of the departed are sure
No matter what contestants will.

Futility is not its own champion.
There are no winners in excess, mostly ignorant hordes.

All succumb regardless of station.
Records of investments and sustainable returns last in people,
perspectives, and promise.

Fear not the future, all share it.

Foundations

Solid, immovable, anchored, firm,
Shaken, crumbling, cracked, or destroyed,

Those constructed with enduring materials, dedicated
    workmanship, and fortified wills,
Withstand any crisis.

What of survival?
    Though not guaranteed,
    It is possible.

Foundations well-formed, remain.
    Diligence,
        Endurance,
            Resolve,
                Focus,
                    Determination,
All live in truth.

What or who secures your structures?

Forging their ways through economic onslaughts, perils,
    discouragements, and disillusionments,
    Downs
        Turn.

Few remain standing.

Freedom's Recompense

Requested for payment,
Preferred in design,
Freedom's recompense,
Contributions' loftier rewards,

Compositions herein formulated,
Bearing strange markings,
Unreadable to most,
Expressed nonetheless,

Pure, isolated,
Purposely align
Nearly to perfection
With the moment and its gifts.

    Freedom light, expressions of hope and evidence
        Emerging from within or without,
  Are yours to enjoy, proclaim, and distribute unreservedly.

Unabashed though misunderstood
A discoverer's journey portrays
Strong character as it charts its course.
Equalinmeaning,intentionalitysatiatesinquiryasmaturitycomes.

Freed men's souls treasure and teach these truths.

Fulfillment

To know fulfillment is a primal longing.
  Its obligations must be met, its doubts overcome.
  Offenses, while they matter, must not prohibit completion of
    termed and timed obligations.
  Blessings, though enjoyed, render neither influence nor
    power beyond the moment.
  Verified meaning defies formulas—it relies on personal
    application.

Conquests do not suffice.
Friendships, regardless of origin, do not qualify, nor do personalities.
Fulfillment is more.

At its core, it is personal. It is
  Untied to outside influence,
  Intimate, shared with but a few,
  Ultimate, fully embraced by its owner exclusively,
  Unlimited, diversely revealed, presented uniquely though
    fashioned by internal rules of engagement.

It cannot be defined with certainty.
  One size assuredly does not fit all.
  Align person, motive, era, and place within collected
    opportunity.
  To each is given a chance to change an outcome, design a
    destiny, leave a legacy, and alter history.

Committed followers position timing, talent, and task.
    While principles endure, applications differ.
    They should.
    They will.
    They command allegiance whenever agreements bind them.

Whose definitions will you adopt?
    Whose meanings will you adapt as precursors or referees?
    Strength comes not from following the crowd;
    Rather, in creating individual goals unalterably tied to
        eternity's laws.
    A birthplace of consummation exists in you.

Gentle Rain

Tapping, a tempo, droplets' tempered scenes,
    Rhythms timed to nobler means,

Acts of God, embrace the whole,
    Freed, detached from man's control.

Water's levels, flowing down,
    Seek a placement, not renown.

From a grander, gloried sight,
    Runs' cascades submit, rewrite

Rain's descending, giving, sending
    Purer, freshened airs unending.

Grains of Sand Alone

Cast away, refined, aged,
Constrained longer than anticipated,
Ultimately released, inquiring,
Wondering, relating,
Piercing lightly wound confines
Hurriedly applied in conditional realities,
Wisdom flourishes.
Penetrated, crevasses of the mind cherish meaning and will
　　for more.

Balanced, weighted icons borne unconventionally
Require sure-footed,
Measured steps.
Those who've slept
Respond little to changing and challenging winds.
Contemplative, their dreamy bliss
Bless few or none of any of this.
Timed treasures surge meaninglessly by, missing them.

Marking its rounds,
Secure within itself,
Knowledge fits cause's requisites.
Fulfilled obligations seek their own levels.
Breaks, breads, beads, and beverages
Refresh perspectives, alternately placed.
Equilibrium commands an observer's obedience.
Gained rest renews and balances recompense.

Ringed, passages dreamt ascend, smoky, spent, consumed,
Yet enriched where happiness reigns
Mid changing times,
Weaving, interlacing creatures and creations together,
Nourishing the body.
Soulfully receive measured sustenance from their confluence.
Hungrily consume the vital nutrients your being craves.
Enjoy respite's refrain, then move on.

Gratitude

Gratitude, an attitude, is difficult if not impossible to measure.
When offerings freely given
Are graciously received,
Both giver and receiver
Experience degrees of hospitality
At levels neither fully comprehend.

At one and identical times
Gifts and presence,
Revealed acts, expressions of kindness
Represent authentic relationships
Rising above triviality's temporal conditions.
These touch timeless dimensions.

Therein reign portions of The Divine.
Few words, if any,
Completely relate
Generosity and receptivity
At heights where no one keeps records of rights or wrongs
And accounts are neither causes nor concerns.

Benefit another and be the other benefited.
Here, in this place of exchange
Where human and eternal forces intersect,
Divorced of encumbrance, shared within their hallowed
    intercourse,
Influential, transforming opportunities born not of this world
Are destined to affect it.

Illumination

Thoughts, desires, well-planned courses,
Viewpoints, truths, and vested sources
Suffer disrepair, closeted disintegration
When lights grow dim and darkness comes.

Withholding blessings, aloof as stone,
Quelling striving's pace, alone,
Potential bides its time, waiting to be born.
Illumination shifts its gaze to those who are most needful.

Ills suffered-long must fade, decay
When long nights turn toward dawning's ray.
Those who've grasped hope, stir, prepare
In full anticipation.

Timeless treasures, stilled, near death
Tended to, receive new breath.
When, as knowledge beams fresh light
Life's rebirths itself once more.

Immortalized

Nameless, insignificant, famous for a time but now overlooked,
Tantalizingly trivial, eventually and forcibly cast aside,
Wild, childish, foreign, and unruly designers could not conceive
How their puny imaginations, displayed in boring delivery,
Wringing surly devastations from plotted schemes,
Some accidentally but most with intent, masking interpretations,
Have been immortalized forever.

If they only knew: little if any were discarded.
Instead, they were inserted into tightly fitting,
Form- and function-revealing contexts,
Places where their circus-wrought spectacles purposefully have
    been recalled to make a point.
Lost, long-forgotten are the characters themselves.
Masses oft have heard, learned, and reviewed their stories.
Willing or not, the trashed, buried, and rotten offerings of these
    deluded malcontents have taught the very lessons they never
    embraced.

Were these performers even remotely aware
They would stop, questioning, blink and stare,
And blink again, though barely cognizant.
Nothing would change.
Events, causes, and caustic results
Remain indefinitely,
Instructing others what not to do.

In the Eyes of a Child

Long before words are formed,
Hearing, comprehension completed,
Known, assured,
Tenderly, eyes speak,

Smiles grace countenances,
Universal, soul-languages,
Of heart, body, and mind
At levels none remember

But all recall,
Evidenced in newer lives
Lovingly caressed,
Securely warmed, anticipating their next opportunity.

Written in 2009 in honor of Gavin, my grandson.

In the Silence

Voices bearing golden truths, even barely distinguishable ones,
    do not emerge from measured wind and vocal cords alone.
Messages that open the mind, move the body, and refresh the
    soul come via multiple means.
Silence, one of many teachers, reveals unfathomed dimensions
    of reality if permitted to speak.

Where calmed and quiet attention, allowed and encouraged,
    focuses energies on revelations not easily disclosed,
    living understanding rises toward significance.
Emotions dwell here, too.
Soul-birthed feelings not punctuated with needless
    interruptions bear fruits of eternal lineage, lasting beyond
    today in unimaginable and unfathomable discoveries
    available to all who create time for fuller saturation in
    artistically laden hopes and dreams, visions and ideals.

What of conversations?
Some of the most meaningful occur when words
    are never uttered.
Communication, pure, precious, treasured and worth preserving
    permeates still spaces.

        Find the silence.
        Form the solace.
        Enjoy their presence.
        Teach their ways.

Inspiration

Undisclosed sources,
None quantified,
Driven by longing,
Art's songs inside,

Coming as wishes,
Living in dreams,
Furthered by talents,
Weighed in what seems,

Welcomed, requested,
Purposed, required,
Piercing the common,
Living, desired,

This is the magic
Worked through its toil:
Ere seeds are planted
Remains but soil.

Render allegiance,
Dwell beyond norms.
Give place, due credence,
Shatter old forms.

Altered paths, chosen,
Change patterns staid.
Uplifted thinking
Freed, shall pervade.

Guests are invited,
Honored once more.
Come, kindred spirits,
Walk through my door.

FREEDOM LIGHT

Interest

Hearkening to an uncovered, naked soul,
Longing eyes,
Cries of the heart,
Softened fingers lingering, returning,

Surpassing superficial expressions,
In loving memories refresh the weary.

Contrary, perfunctory admonitions
Displaying surface-abiding demands, do not suffice.
Pulsating, non-guessing expressions of love
Evoking keener desires,

Born, silenced, and dying to rise again,
Compose varied purposes for which they're destined, and
    speak volumes.

Where passions are piqued
Pleasant invitations punctuate routine environments.
Non-shifting sands bid the transient to build and dwell.
These counteract waves of turmoil sure to come with more than
    simple wishes.

Interest begets widening perspectives,
Searching unknowns, discovering peace.

Keep the Dream Alive

Keep the dream alive
In your heart, in your soul,
Don't give up on the prize,
Keep your eyes on the goal.

> When the journey is true,
> Then it's all up to you
> To pursue, carry on,
> It's your life.

Keep the dream alive
Walk the road you must choose,
With your faith as your guide
Run the race, win or lose.

> When the journey is true,
> God will bless it for you.
> It's your dream, it's your cause,
> It's your life.

> Challenges come,
> Tears multiply,
> But with love on your side
> You'll continue to try.

GLEN AUBREY

Keep the dream alive
Overcome any fear.
Standing strong, face the wrong,
Never quit, persevere.

                When the journey is true,
                  Then it's all up to you
                    To pursue, carry on,
                        It's your life.

        Some say, "You can't,"
        Others, "You could."
        You'll achieve what you must
        'Cause you know that you should.

Keep the dream alive
In your heart, in your soul,
Don't give up on the prize,
Keep your eyes on the goal.

                When the journey is true,
                God will bless it for you.
            It's your dream, it's your cause,
                      It's your life.

Used with permission.

FREEDOM LIGHT

Keep the Dream Alive

Words and Music by Glen Aubrey

1. Keep the dream a-live in your heart, in your soul, don't give up on the prize, keep your eyes on the goal. When the journey is true, then it's all up to you to pursue, carry on, it's your life.

2. dream a-live, walk the road you must choose, with your faith as your guide, run the race, win or lose. When the journey is true, God will bless it for you. It's your dream, it's your cause, it's your life. 2. Keep the

Copyright © 2009 Glen Aubrey.
All Rights Reserved. Printed in U.S.A.

GLEN AUBREY

Labels

Labels don't apply.
Mistake-ridden descriptions, faulty instructions, false information
Fail to align with content or intent.
Flaking, this tag's glue no longer holds.

Confused, the minute thwarts the monumental,
Draws energies away from the vitally important,
Dwarfing focused and more profitable ends in immaterial,
    culturally-driven inhibitions,
Inventories of uncomfortable, misapplied associations and
    conditional excuses.

Newly minted versions are placed into old and broken boxes for
    safekeeping,
Treasuring that which when exposed
Limits its potential, consumes its container,
And voids its warranty, expressed or implied.

Peel these meaningless labels off, shred them.
Ill-constructed and misconstrued definitions,
Caring little for continuity or continuation,
Prove inaccurate o'er time, passing due dates.

        Discard and destroy them
    Else they contaminate more than they should.

Learned Once More

No degrees of thorough planning could prepare for this.
The brightest minds have failed.
Their fortunes missed enduring and destiny-altering truths,
Those gained only through observation that learning the
　　lessons of history's collections provides.

Ignorance bodes no sustainable bliss.
Naivete-impaled,
An era's sad reflection's mist
Requires truths to be taught and received by newer
　　populations endowed with fresh directives, founded on
　　principles that endure.

Learning

Others, The Teachers, the living instructors,
    Courageously impassioned, have imparted truth to you.

The eager learner continually craves for these associations.
    Possessing genuine receptivity, relishing knowledge and
        wisdom, ones with open minds attract interconnection
        with like-minded souls.

Remember
    The professor mindful enough to listen and offer help,
    The parent who set aside special times to be with you alone,
    The grandparent who answered your curious questions
        without contempt,
    The sibling who kept your heart's secrets, and helped you
        through your crises,
    The friend who agreed, promised, and then delivered,
    The God Who remained faithful when you were not,
    The clergy who cared enough to ask how you were doing,
    The pets that comforted you in ways no human could,
    The child who taught truths far beyond their years,
    The unnamed persons who from a distance freely shared
        their hard-won treasures,
    The counselor who loved you enough to honestly deal with
        issues that mattered?

These instructed in times and means unique to each of them.
    Their classrooms differed widely.

Esteem them for who they were
    Even more than for what they gave.

Understand that what you've gained
    Has altered life forever.

Lengthening Shadows

Fleeting twilight
Gone births one night
Next morning's light
Revealed despite

Travel's finished
Twice replenished
Strongholds grasped then
Formed what had been

Up becomes down
Losses renown
Fomenting change
Views rearrange

Minds held secure
Valued endure
World's turning views
Sifted as news

Close up a grave
Lives may it save
Endings of one
Bless life begun

FREEDOM LIGHT

Linger

Timed and placed,
Treasured beyond the ordinary,
Connecting beneath and above surfaced courtesies,
Serenity bids a traveler to rest.

Linger here.

Savor a soulful embrace's sweetest joys.

Relish the purer blessing
Alive in essence, plentiful.
Celebrate unending favors.
Abide in the energies of love.

Live to Last

Story's ending
Bears its past,
Final chapters
Written, last.

Strong convictions
Locked, unmoved,
Frame opinions
Held then proved.

This collection
Opened, closed,
Crafted, patterned
Views composed.

Storytelling,
Tales of old
Narrate lessons
Ancients told.

Exercising
Knowledge then
Anchors truth to
Action when

Living studies
Learned may be
Evidenced in
Legacy.

Lonesome Grace

A lonesome grace
Though out of place,
Forgiveness-laced,
Heartthrob-replaced,

    Long-suffered wrongs
    Where right belongs,
    Wrought duties fail,
    Past debts prevail.

        Remembrance brings
        Forgotten stings
        Where hopes for one
        Bear pains not done.

            These seek a peace,
            A pure release
            Where new abodes
            Bear lightened loads.

                A longing's zeal,
                Dawn's fresh appeal
                Projected, viewed,
                See life renewed.

                    Perspectives race
                    Voids to displace,
                    So bygone years
                    Bring fewer tears.

Longing

Eagerly sought,
Passionate expression pours forth, unhindered.
Eyes speak,
Gestures compel,
Tentative steps respond.
Longings of the heart embrace intimacy, and love.

Expectantly focused on brighter futures,
Hopes arise, meet, and conjoin.
Softer touches
Close absences, heal abscesses.
Relating stories of war borne wounds and shattered wills, those
    who grieve and those who care welcome restoration.
Consummation's tenderness flows, absent inhibition.

Enter dimensions heretofore imagined, yet believed.
Corollary movements, fondest interactions,
Points secured, secretive, gently assured,
Repair brokenness, realign companionship,
And mend isolated, hurting souls.

Loss

Loss of priceless treasure moves inward reflections to burrow
    deeper, sorrowing,
Abandoning the present to address more urgent tyrannies.

Absent loftier vision's bearing, where faith's eternal hopes are
    brought closer to the breast,
Despair would surely reign until convincingly replaced by nobler
    themes.

Imagination ponders its past and forecasts its future.
Perspectives become clearer when viewed holistically than when
    considered in unresolved isolationism.

Inclusive grief, tender relief
Combine within primal existence.

Memory's Chords

Rich harmony's surging melodies,
Interlocking and complimentary,
Resonate, penetrate, and permeate ordinary environments,
Proclaim an august presence,
And present personal invitations toward mysterious habitations
Wherein senses respond
Above and beyond the common
As if hearkening to another life's calling.

Personhood is heard here,
Not observed within scenes chosen by connecting lines
    randomly;
Rather, purposefully,
Known only to their performers.
Bearers, listeners, expositors,
Who through confusion and clutter
Still recognize the value of the soul,
Reproduce gentler, more precious, time-honored masterpieces,
    calling their owners homeward, bound.

Joyfully invading present proclivities,
Renewing life's original, long-forgotten forms,
Warmth's receptions await fresh entrances.
Come they will, uninvited or planned, so invite them.
Protected within cherished repositories:
The phrase of a song, the touch of a hand, the call of longing eyes,
Fine wines embellishing a dinner for two, assuring, friendly smiles,
Affections enlivened toward awakened awareness, respond.

GLEN AUBREY

Chords satiate a room
As recollections birthed anew
Enrich most cherished friendships,
Sweeten the memories of treasured places,
Encourage approaches of peaceful reunion,
Relish pursuits of soulful happiness,
And invigorate the inner core.
Lifted, a being cries from her heart, "You are home."

Monuments

Stone monuments,
Enduring sentinels, erect, honoring achievement,
Do not outlast defining sacrifice,
Recalled in faithful service.

Memories dwell in minds and marble,
Virtues in eternal souls.
Legacy rewards the latter.
Ages keep their sacred tolls.

More than Hope

Passing hope,
>Views require,
>Vision sees,
>Souls inspire.

Wishes, dreams
>Weakly prayed,
>Resting, stilled,
>Slowly fade.

Strong desires
>Firmly laid
>Persevere,
>Never swayed.

Choices made,
>Actions bold,
>Turn mere dross
>Into gold.

Morning Comes

A rotating earth presents fresh opportunities
Every twenty-four hours.

Clothed in conflict, peace, or blight,
Discord, concord, wrong, or right,

Morning comes.

Night passes because it must.
Light infuses heretofore unidentified options, foreordained.

Refuse recognition of these displays?
Complacency condemns a day's potential.

Morning comes.

Purposed plans pursued
Reveal futures once foretold.

Rest and striving in symbiotic accord
Mark a day's treasures, but not impassively.

Morning comes.

Music

An apex,
Meticulously supported mid swelling undercurrents,
Ascending, piercing its boundaries, returning home,

Sustained, fluid,
Motioninghands,breaths,andmindstowardcooperativeharmonies,
Blending timing, effects, moods, and cadence,

Questioning, answering, cajoling, persuading,
Pursuing purer melodic and rhythmic interludes,
Finding essence, seeking personality, conversing with itself,

Resides alone.
Others join.
A song is born.

Music Is Stirring

Music surrounds us, touching our souls, reaching the depths of our beings.
Creation's connections transcend any written description.

Fine's compositions come in varying ways: a dawning is but one.
A relationship's strivings pervade each morning's scenes as passages ebb and flow.

Quiet the needless, disturbing distractions.
Stifle the stories that tear hearts apart.

Relate the breathless, romantic tales, adapting their melody's freedom dance.
Art attracts, blends, and nurtures what altered themes portray.

While some refuse this music's offerings, hastening away,
Fresh minds compose and express novel forms, alive in new patterns, exceeding old norms.

Melodies thrive o'er contemptuous struggling,
Inspiring those who listen well, few though they be.

Freely extended, brilliantly adorned, technically flawless, ruggedly individual, supporting essence while balancing poetry's intent,
Performances replay within the mind, a magnificent auditorium, admired by all who enter and partake.

Emotions conducted without reservation or obstruction are refreshed.
Wonder is their product.

Accept, do not ask why.
Write, play, sing, embrace.

Love's release
Goes forth, assured.

Worth, venerated, regenerates the artist as well as her recital.
These are required for beings to rise above the routine.

Nearly Persuaded

Nearly persuaded to
      Take the step
      Make the call
      Mail the letter
      Write the piece
      Sound the alarm
      Respond to love
      Enter a room
      Approach the course
      Talk it through
      Plumb the depths
      Try once more

Contemplation moves one to choose.
Conviction dwells within occasion.
Who convinces whom?
Who will follow and obey?

Almost never is not traction.
Formed, a thought is not its action.

Pushed, encouraged toward completion,
Matters pondered of the heart,
Stake their claims mid mounting risk,
Compelling one to start.

No Words

Soul-infused, diligence-driven, yet compliant,
Burdensome, lengthy, lonesome hours progress
As workers yearn to reap their justly earned rewards.

Ever-present tensions, struggling contrasts,
Sentiments strung tightly between connected yet opposing world views
Seek expanding recognition, trophies earned, and men's applause.

Investors seek a balance of achievements and their names.
Striving, never giving up, efforts are not restrained, nor should they be for the greater good.
Urges toward obtaining validation of a higher cause remain fixed, intentional, focused, and assured.

An artisan portrayals expressly try conflicting motives, to frame disruption's discontent in universal realms.
Grateful souls intently look to more than what they see,
In time returning abundance-laden, celebrating unconstrained.

There are no words to describe this homecoming.

FREEDOM LIGHT

Now

    Not then

        Not when

            Nor if

Not should

        Not could

            Nor perhaps

Now Is

        Presence

            Being

Now Is

        Humanity

            Wondrously alive in freedom's light

Destiny prepares us as we would fashion its foundation,
Intertwining souls, spirits, minds, flesh, beliefs, discussion, and compatibilities.

Compose this now.
Refuse excuses.

Forgive the past.
Dwell presently.

Return the gifts revered, entrusted,
Valued greater than before.

Working toward fulfilling dreams,
Celebrate these wonders wrought when comes their consummation.

Now Is

    You and me

        Facing opportunity

Occupying Space, Spending Time

Phase's lesser wishes, discarded through life's transitions,
Expend treasures fruitlessly, spurning God-breathed
　　opportunities.
Moments thus consumed return few chances for enrichment.
Profitable enterprises submerged here, emerge elsewhere for
　　another.

A day's passage is used but once.
Payments appear, singularly fulfilling wise investments.
Legacy's profits clearly defined, agreed, performed,
Live unshackled by coincidence.

Occupying space, spending time,
Divorced from defined objectives
Showcase flagrant self absorption.
Sickening wastes restrain success.

Now occurs, emboldened where reflections linger, as do their
　　effects.
Occupy intentionally.
Pay with purpose.
Sure recompense comes in your life or another's.

Opportunity

Captured, challenged, changed, and deliberately
    re-manufactured,
Formerly deterred mixes, synergistic matches
Reside in realms of the imagination
Until released to blend cooperating ingredients once more.

Superseding them, initiative assumes control.
Superior manifestations break traditions' stale, disgusting
    molds.
Conflicts of wills are silenced
When lasting perspectives stimulate permanence, guiding.

Benefits received, worth far more than the costs of their
    acquisition,
Prove reliability, especially when the chips are down.
People, promises, plans, and processes
Reproduce the unbelievable out of the ordinary.

Twin peaks share similar parentage but differ widely.
Compare composition and character.
Against backgrounds initially appearing out of focus, clarified,
Opportunity emerges for those who diligently strive.

Passing on the Bridge

Passing on the bridge,
A solitary lane,
Windows' shades compel a soul
Mid whispered invitations
To fill a heart's desire,
Reach unearthly consummations,
Freed, content, fulfilled, serene, rested, and renewed,
Cleansing long held anguish from the heart.

Deep-seated pain's grief-stricken souls,
Bathed in cooling waters where one stops,
Pauses for refreshment,
Breathes renewal's air,
Wander oft between their dreams and life's difficult realities.
Replenishment absorbs a broken spirit, mends the mind, revives
    the core.
Touched, the wounds begin to heal.
A being is restored.

FREEDOM LIGHT

Persuasion, Permission, Perspective

The View commands attention
When its seers are overcome.

Penetrating eyes, attentive, listening ears, limbs advancing
 freely in cooperating probes,
Attend to abstract voices when their owners are secure.

Persuasiontowardacceptanceopensminds,freeswillinghearts.
Revelations, with permission from inquirers of the truth, teach
 lessons never learned, prevented until now.

When firm beliefs of someone cause another to ask why,
Perspectives broaden living, birth decisions, as they should.

Those who enter earnestly are better for their choice,
No matter length of processes, regardless of the voice.

Profound Expressions

Complex imagery, intriguingly diverse, entertaining all the senses,
Composes expressions, interwoven parts, fascinating dialogues
Commanding the attentions of thoughtful persons,
Engaged individuals who sever constricting bonds of ease and mediocrity in their expanding quests for more.

They number few who do.
Achievers do not relinquish proven promises or permanent premises;
Instead, they delight in mastery,
Excel in creativity.

Impetus and initiative reign in the hearts of earnest searchers
Though they share a lone existence.
Like leadership at the top,
Internal consummation reveals strengths in isolation.

Calls for exploration require agreeable responses
From longing ones who enthusiastically participate in life-altering, momentous treasure hunting.
Those who infuse artistically-driven genius into unencumbered desires for enrichment
Add value to their concepts as well as contributions.

Trifles are weighed against worthwhile expectations
Usually pushed down and back,
Proven immaterial, or so it may seem
Until expressed in another time and a better place.

Unquenchable questioners abide
As do diligent ones who complete their tests,
Continually examining the answers to life's supreme and
    immeasurably significant interrogatories, then asking why the
    conclusions they've been taught are worthy of their sanction.
Responders willingly and without reservation love to learn, then
    teach other students who, like them, desire to live in truth.

Quiet Contemplation

In quiet contemplation
Welcomed respite from long and lonely undertakings
Cradles nuances of distant, though renewed perspectives,
Seldom seen.

Often dimmed by the din of a hundred distractions and
Meaningless encroachments,
Purpose, marred by infelicitous reactions of a faith, so called,
Looses relevance amid the drones of countless, restless crowds.

Alone is a state of mind—a place of intentional being—
A presence where uninhibited thoughts yearn to live in freedom,
    birthing offspring.
If presented with uninterrupted opportunities,
Needs for rest are matched with nature's best.

          May it be?
     The beauty of a garden
      The solace of a home
    The shadows of a sunset
      The glory of the sky
     The majesty of morning
    The wonder of new birth

Communion,
Wine for the soul and bread for the body
Offers promise of hope for tomorrow.
In the stillness of this sacred place refreshment waits for you.

Rescue

Define it.
It is used or abused.

Controls, condescension, blatant subversiveness, bizarre and unseemly behaviors
Beg for heroic intrusions.

Stinging, obligatory, unnatural, and tenaciously indecorous tendencies
Predictably request more than can be paid.

Positive consequences accompany neither efforts nor effects.
Leave it alone—this handout is not your obligation or responsibility.

Restful Recompense

After the labors of the day, restful recompense, uninhibited, free,
Marks trusted, truth-tested, untamed relations,
Friendships unfiltered, undaunted, re-placed,
Where foolhardy objections of former jealous and insecure
    acquaintances, fail.

Cherish preserved, validated dreams.
Mold ideas, rend the seams
Where strictures lie.
Squelch negativity, let it die.

Contemplation craves courteous discourse where receptivity
    and response are respected and upheld.
Released from low esteem, ceaseless mistrusting, inflamed
    egos run amuck, and intimidation's floundering formulas,
Rise, conquering, confidently assured.
Live within gracious environments you only imagined existed, but
    were convinced in your heart were true.

Return

Venture home, re-enter what you've known.
Bright yellow ribbons tied to oaks, adorn your front yard.
This homecoming is but one event in life's repeating cycles.
Join the celebration and renew acquaintance-ties.

Decide your times and places, conditions of return.
Anticipate that others might not see, and may not learn.

Rebounding from a fall,
Relive adventures bold,
Rejoin your vital causes,
Replace with warmth the cold.

Restored, a loving brotherhood
At points, means go alone.
You must walk a highway
Till you come into your own.

Memories rekindled
Of what went right or wrong
Call for your perspectives
Expressed where you belong.

GLEN AUBREY

Shown for composition,
Return is not rebirth.
This may be no more or less
Than standing on your earth.

Welcome home
    If home is where your heart is
        And there you dwell in peace.

Rocking Chairs and Scented Candles

Rocking chairs and scented candles recall faded, yet peculiar tales
Where distant memories, once collected then preserved,
Offer comforts or regrets,
Pervading depths of soul.

Fireplace recitals, wondering, earnest eyes
Search sequestered meanings, long forgotten but alive,
Sealing older hearts and stealing younger minds,
While pets, obliged, oblivious, meld comfort with desire.

Softer music's lofty themes comprise uplifting realms
Where thinking of what could have been
Replaces, for a time, fraught and harsh realities.
With hopes for bright tomorrows, there is nothing firm, secure.

Rapture's reminiscences captured, tightly held,
Merge with flavored, favored dreams
As age progresses on and on, creeping uninvited,
Swallowing inhibitors and graces without pause.

Profit's wonders' haughty splurge,
Self-wrought plunder's greedy urge,
Human blunder's righteous scourge,
Form effects that shall emerge.

    Reflections of the ancient's past become the tales retold
      In lives of other people, the new, the young, the old.

Scenes

Ubiquitous chances,
Depth's perceptions,
Encouraging, casual, outward glances
Mixing and churning in soulful regions, though unkept,
Heretofore closed off but newly bursting with promise,
Timely and tempered, attuned to owners and their keep, alive in maturation's necessities,
Push pleasantries to expand and contract.

Rhythmic pulsations breathe beneath tempered performances,
Permeating multi-layered surfaces notwithstanding distractions,
Opening environs long unobserved until unearthed.
Tasted delicacies, savored through abundance graciously expressed,
Measure worth's common and scaled templates, aligning to alternate grading systems.
Freeing themselves from encumbrances, lessening burdens, gazing upward,
Ones not content with conditions that are, focus intently on what must become.

Superior contents fill abandoned spaces to their brims.
Platforms so designed inspire authors to reach for unheard-of
>>heights,
Enthralling interested passers by, annoying malcontents.
Enraptured, inquisitive ones saturate sensitized and sensuously
>>hungry vacuums.
Verity'slongevitythriveswithinladenyetfreedrealmssimultaneously.
Offspring's strengths inspire ancient, enduring meditations.
Ash's impurities breed a ground's rebirth as newer scenes unfold.

Seeking for More

Loneliness,

    Longing,

        Learning,

            Loving

Merge within recesses of the heart and mind and soul.

    Gratify but one, the rest are fast affected.

        Warmed embrace's sure delights

            Shall satisfy the whole.

Loneliness falters where friendships are proved.

    Longing is filled where a vacuum's removed.

        Learning increases where openness reigns.

            Loving is essence where life-force remains.

Snow

Ascended, apart,
Majestic, serene,
Intricate forms
Strangely complex,

Secretive, visiting briefly,
Vanishing, falling, uplifted,
Submitting,
Come again, predicted or not.

Appearances,
Crystallizations
Softly blanketing hardening crusts,
Peacefully floating, or wantonly invading,

Gathered, shaped,
Finessed in crafted frames,
Exist beyond reach or measure.
Probing eyes merely scan their collective compositions.

No two alike, each resembles the other.
Separate births, cooperative strengths,
Coexisting as friends or foes in formidable habitats,
Their powers offer warnings alongside welcomed views.

GLEN AUBREY

Drawing rapt attention from one peak to another,
Mighty mid their flurries, grander in their reign,
Timed, their season's birth and waning
Thrill the guests who come to gaze.

Softer

Assuaging the grief,
Knowing what to say, when or if to speak at all,
Tenderly approaching hurts, identifying origins,
Selfless persons understand, and comfort those in pain.
Softer scenes, serene and sacred
Sanctify communion.

Beauty comes, resides anew, replenished as it grows.
Willing beings, unrestricted,
Open hands, untie their bonds.
Unfettered minds, eager, learning,
Lives released toward meaning, yearning,
Weigh their past, displace detractors, diminish doubts, unlock
  new doors, and fashion alignments of gracious responsibility.

Shared perspectives' connecting points,
Divergent views courteously considered,
Offering help where ties are strong,
Reposition priorities, suiting persons and their causes.
Soul mates are released to love
As they've never been before.

Solemnity

Messages from afar, appearing inconspicuously at first,
Infuse a routine's tiresome tasks with elevated meanings.
Inspiration speaks in ways beyond what normal knows.

Open up the packages presented in surprise,
Remove their complex wrappings, or simple coverings.
Extol your fresh discoveries in sheer exhilaration.

Make way for magic moments, unexpected yet confirmed.
Solemn vows, sacred bows, sacrificial offerings,
Salubrious engagements bear distinctive, timed rewards.

Respond to alterations when they come upon the scene.
Endurance calls, rekindles passions,
Silenced temporarily.

Soon promoted, thriving, rising, festooned for celebrations,
Exceeding the familiar, rote, unremarkable, customary, and
    predictable patterns,
They live outside the common, and change it for the good.

Awesome relevance,
Tidings of great joy
Burst with pride in this dignity's renewal.

Somehow

Somehow here, arrived from there,
Juxtaposed commitments share

Journey's common goals revealed,
Fixed, secured in frame and field.

Mirrors' views, bold futures find
Blended souls in cause combined.

Sovereign

The Infinite, Transcendent,
    To sensory perceptions, foreign,
    Unknowable apart from expressions of faith,
    Offers enticing views of sovereignty's compelling, grand
        enigmas.
    No one lays claim to exalted positions of foreknowledge
        exceeding reality.

Countries, nationalities
Proclaim autonomy yet,
Self-governed cultures, challenged, lost,
Question whether independence ever existed or even could.

An entity's declaration,
"We dwell as sovereign beings"
May one day be proven false
For realms and rights are temporal.

Is ours a self-determined land?
For how long may its frameworks stand?
Who can truly guarantee
A firm sustainability?

Foundations hold a people's state for lengths of times unknown.
How misguided, presumed wise,
Are those proclaiming that their cause
Shall last against Another's will?

Spoken

We speak.
Thoughtried,communication'seffortsseldomreachcompletion.
Refreshed, energized, tested anew, received openly without
 undue criticism,
Perspectives are valued, requested in healthy relationships
 where reckless abandonment is not practiced and original
 ideas are not idly discarded.

Often refused when trust is broken or removed,
It is then one listens deeper.
These thoughts
May not originate with me.

Dialogue at discomforting levels,
Especially when accord is absent and expressions remain
 difficult or confused,
Release intellects to higher degrees of receptivity and greater
 comprehension,
But only when desires for peace exceed controlling means.

Transitional phases come and go,
Teaching, though its ways are tough.
While processes repeat their cycles through any number of
 years,
Well spoken truths endure and outlast wars of wasted breath.

Communal systems' baseborn talks, restrictive, binding rules,
Foster firm resolve in hearts desiring to speak freely,
To acquire fresher air, position pure, unfettered forms.
Expanded understandings, wide imagination's plains, open
    unexplored horizons, compelling brave constituents to share
    their grandest schemes.

Remove thorn-laden barriers of shut and closed off minds.
Tear down needless inhibitions,
Those awash in fear.
Thanks for listening.

Star Struck

When an individual's identity rests within another's persona
Questions interrupt this futility if allowed to be proposed:
"If you chose to be yourself who would you then, be? What new
    views, expanding options opened would you see?"
Innermost character abides within growing personal constructs
    when released to fully form.

Mysteriously powerful discoveries brimming with joyful
    confidence
Await individuals discontent with inferior views of themselves.
Valiant souls destroy formidable walls designed to prevent
    adventuresome explorations,
Refusing blatant, pushy, constrictive efforts from lost, tawdry,
    insecure mentors, ones who encourage their students to
    mimic mediocrity and move insufficiently in experimental
    confines.

Shallowandsurface-dwelling,thetiniesteffortsofthesegrossly
    deficient leaders are thinly rewarded when shown for their
    true compositions.
Unto its own a price is paid.
An essence controls
Foundations laid.

Empty containers produce excessive noise when beaten.
Closed up, abandoned none too soon,
They reveal gross inadequacies—moldy, stark vacuums—
As they horde the atmospheres they fashioned then imposed
 on others.

Open vessels beg to be filled, invite repeated use, seek
 cooperative compatibility.
Owners design this environment's reality.
Open minds and committed hearts reside and grow from here.
Horizons call to all.

Earnest ones, alive to their core constitutions
Embrace each opportunity to mature within themselves,
Welcoming truths they may discover,
Sojourning among those who remain unsatisfied with the status quo.

Sure Rewards

It comes as no surprise,
What's hidden 'neath disguise
Is seen with different eyes
Of one who tests and tries.

Lasting combinations
Outreach contemplations,
More than conversations,
Stirring revelations.

Proofs emerge from action,
Deeds produced through traction.
Quests, your satisfaction
Live in interaction.

The Blank Page

Pen to paper
Nothing came
So I write to
Tell the same

In these poems'
Goals remain
Served intentions
Measured gain

Hoped beginnings
Piece by piece
Unrequited
Till release

Comes upon me
Morning's light
Strength's renewal
Now I'll write

The Chorused Freedom

Knowledge, power, bought then sold,
Wisdom sought by kings,
Fade, compared with simpler truths,
Pleasure's offerings.

Longings linked to precepts shared,
Joining will and mind,
Reign in chorused freedom's realms,
Leaving none behind.

The Old Piano

It rests, tones silenced, hammers stilled, alone, consigned to waiting,
Stored against a furthest wall while fully present in the room
Until the fingers it helped train return to play it once again.
The touch fits like a hand in glove, familiar like an easy chair, while practiced challenge, growth, and pain are still recalled as new.

As fifty years approach their time, a promised guarantee, the sounding board, wood keys, and strings, strongly made, remain.
Indeed, perhaps, this instrument has finally come of age.
Pitches are not tight right now, they vary naturally.
It should be tuned, played gently first, re-entering a phase.

Like close friends gathered carefully, respected, and well treated,
A kinder touch comprises all that's needed for this time.
Composed, rehearsed, repeated oft, its melodies resound,
Still abiding in the heart, the hands, the soul, the mind.

Lengthy, arduous, awkward times of writing, orchestration, methods honed to impact tunes for years and years to come, bring smiles while I recall the works of clients' projects, done.
Brand new roles pianos filled when moved to second stages:
Parts envisioned by design, heard first between the ears,
Were formed, selected, harmonized, then transcribed to pages.

The instrument retains its bench, its pedals work, its stand's
 intact.
Some will pause to share their songs, but keys are known by one
 alone.
Felt and filmed, recorded, played,
It holds both anguish and acclaim.

This piano's not too old, compared to many others.
Yet it breathes through ones who heard its tunes as well as made
 them.
Viewed with reverential awe, or worshipped as an idol?
No, it's still a confidant, and very useful tool.

The Passion

Impassioned souls share rich experiences
With like-minded pilgrims who traverse similar pathways,
Where indifference dies,
Engagement thrives,
And living ones bear their own kind,

Where common fears are tossed away as used up, careworn
    discards,
Soon replaced with innovations crafted by faithful servants'
    hands
Whose fruits of labor endure beyond singularly struggling
    effects.
Stewards of far greater cause give more than what they're given,
Molding portions of their lives with others whom they touch.

The Return

Diminished before the onset of sharpened pangs of birth,
Imagined prior to pre-ordained, rhythmical contractions,
In motion ere initiatives push their earned preeminence,
Indiscriminate returns fall short of expectations.

Unspoken lines of demarcation
Define not wrought intentions.
A commoner's restrictions bind a great explorer's wishes.
Limit this dream's longings and fulfillment is denied.

Cherished ones protect their own.
Heart's desires emerge in view after darkness fades.
Purposeful engagements, positioned and propelled,
Reach beyond mere grasping, freed from inhibitions.

Unplanned payments of a course yield unaccustomed change.
Flowers bloom where planted, and tiny shoots will thrive,
If nourished in their season and destiny agrees.
Harvests surely come; reap what's sown in time.

They Cannot Speak

Pleading expressions,
    Aired feelings,
    Unscripted lines,
    Unrestricted vulnerability,
Laced with dignity,
    Request recognition when spoken language fails.

Silent tongues,
    Communication subject to intentional interpretation,
    Purposeful listening at levels not dependent on hearing
        alone,
    Core understandings,
Minus unnecessary and therefore unfruitful verbiage,
    Demand uncommon, unfamiliar methods of receptivity.

Genuine interests
    Birth ingenuity,
    Design implementation,
    Participate in doing.
Misrepresentations dwindle as they should.
    Formerly and customarily accepted, excuse-driven
        barriers are destroyed and their debris is swept
        away, dumped.

    If they cannot speak or choose to utter naught,
        Listen with your soul to what they say.

This Time

This time will be different, amended, undefiled,
Justified, authentic, completed, destined, pure.

What assures the fruit that any cause should see?
Naught secures an outcome, and this is truth well spoken.

Lines rehearsed behind the curtain ready the performer.
Weigh these planned presenters against others unprepared.

Parties who cooperate venture long together.
Resting on assurances they strive to win their dreams.

Upon what they might agree,
Upon what they must forebear,

Upon what they view through mists,
Mark the patterns of their faith.

Less has much toward saving face; rather more to saving grace,
Blinded to environments apart from what they know.

Kindle fires, fan their flames,
Else untended they grow cold.

Time rests not exclusively in hands of those who use it.
Claim its opportunity in hearts and minds or lose it.

GLEN AUBREY

Who will grasp these moments, making times their own?
Now may be an only chance to plant, then reap what's sown.

Time

We can't go back.
In present states
Our future lives
Unmask our fates.

    We learn from what was and abide in what is,
      Planning for all that may yet come to pass.

Times foreordained
In stones, are cast.
Achievements won
In people, last.

A chance to win
Scorned, squandered, lost
Is weighed within
Eternal cost.

Resolved once more
Re greater cause,
Proposed new plans
Rescind old laws.

As clocks wind down,
As moments wane,
Effects reveal
Each loss or gain.

Uncloudeded Eyes

Of innumerable roads
But one is preferred.

Deciding then choosing
If vision is blurred,

Hearing positions,
Opinions shared,

Clarifies naught
To the vision-impaired.

To pick your course justly,
To reach for your prize,

Call faith to action
With unclouded eyes.

Those who through striving
Achieve what they must,

Listen intently
To persons they trust.

Welcomed Home

The ways back, in abundance,
Represent sundry varieties from which to select.
Each cherishes singular, enchanted hopes.
These adorn the worthy and worthless alike.

                               Awash in grateful recognition,
                                     Honored guests,
Those who've paid the price and endured more than their share
                                   Return to cheer and goodwill.

Sorted tasks' sordid pasts
Mark tales of despairing ones.
Suffered journey's sorties die alone in memory's crypts.
Stake no claim upon unrequited joys.

                                          A picket gate,
                                        Arms opened, wait.
                                        Sad, wearied souls
                                            Anticipate.

Left to chance,
Or purposed, sent,
Forgiven saints
Come home, though spent.

                                        A welcomed place
                                        Extends its space,
                                          Creates a room,
                                          A stronger grace.

GLEN AUBREY

For far too long
Have wanderings
Consumed you
And those who love you still.

Comfort's rests shall fill your soul.
A bold request is honored.

Well Done

Sweeping generalizations leave keen and inquisitive
 intelligences cold, uninterested, isolated, stricken,
Questioning motive, and formulating exits.

Strategic thinking, mindfully aware of layered communication,
Beckons ones to pause, look, listen, linger, learn meanings, and
 refine their methodology.

Satisfaction indwells completed assignments,
Present in health, dignity, purer pride, and the acknowledgements
 of purposed actions brought to term.

Salvation honors the blessed and shapes the blessings of a
 worker's faith and faithfulness.
Well done.

Were It Not So Different

I'd use words to reach you here

    I'd release another tear

        I'd approach to draw you near

            I'd embrace what we hold dear

I'd compose a sweeter song

    I'd forgive a greater wrong

        I'd submit so we'd belong

            I'd do right instead of wrong

Are these but fleeting fantasies,

    Futilities retained,

        Unreachable solutions,

            Or wishes never gained?

No, these emerge from longings found to ring in truth.

Change the title, fix your gaze.

Play your versions, mark your days.

Pen your story lines anew.

Grow where grace and faith renew.

When What Is Dreamt

When what is dreamt but is not proved
Become essentials then removed

When what is treasured in the mind
Become stale wishes left behind

When what is told, recalled, though pained
Become remembrances detained

When what is sung in joyful tune
Become gray mists that hide the moon

When what is shared in living poor
Become the bolts that lock the door

When what is lived, dire memories
Become dysfunctions no one sees

When what is lost in daunting spells
Become the lies their story tells

Then look to One Whose love can purge
A core from sin's repulsive scourge.

Once forgiven, His embrace
Redeems a soul and offers grace.

When, Where, Why, How

When from victor's triumphs
Shall emerge forgiven wrongs?

Where from voices silenced
Shall resound pure, sweeter songs?

Why to soulful yearnings
Shall fulfillments never come?

How with wanton sadness
Must a mortal chant be dumb?

Afterword

Conclusions are not final. This side of eternity they are subject to receipt of new information, developing degrees of understanding, and continuous evaluation.

Inquisitive minds accept little, apart from the basics, on the basis of another's explorations or experience. Individual searching supersedes pre-imposed or presupposed answers which, in expanded analysis, fall short.

I do not know what I do not know. Resting on what I believe, however, born of proven principle and practice, I recognize fully that some truths are unshakable. I also realize that there are immensely vast bodies of information that I will not be able to assimilate, much less communicate in ten completed lifetimes.

Given the fact that all of humankind possesses but one life in which to define ultimate truth, inquisitive ones waste little time or energy pursuing nonessential engagements or entertainments that may not advance greater understanding and communication of knowledge and wisdom.

With hope for your successful venture, possessing evidence that the journey is the destination, may you experience your sojourn with others who care, those with whom you joyfully share your enterprise, its dreams, frustrations, desires, struggles, advances, and declines. Along the way be assured of this fact: You bring worth to every single moment of inquiry because you are more valuable than what you do. Whether or not conclusive answers are realized during your lifetime, you are enriched because of the efforts you make.

Marvel not that you hunger or search for expanded information to enhance and guide your life. Appreciate that God has gifted you with intelligence and an inquiring mind. Use your intellect. Enrich your education. Exercise continual quests to learn what you do not know. Teach others to do the same.

Enjoy your journey. Grow.

More than can be imagined is at stake. From what you receive you will construct storehouses of treasures that are yours to freely give away.

Herein is fulfillment.

Long for new information.
Listen to individuals who are wiser than you.
Learn from a few of them.
Love unreservedly.
Laugh often.
Lessen the burden of the downtrodden.
Live in freedom light.

Leave a positive, enduring legacy in the lives of others.

Your contributions will live through people you may never know.

Acknowledgements

Life is a gift from God. I treasure it and honor the people who share it with me. There are many.

Here I wish to name two individuals who have contributed to the success of this venture. I offer sincere appreciation to Jordan Peck, Acquisitions Editor of Creative Team Publishing, for her tireless efforts expended in the editing processes. She is a treasure. Her work is wonderful. She is a joy.

To my son, Justin Aubrey, I express my sincere thanks for the magnificent art work that composes the front and back covers of this book. His artistic gifts amaze me. He is man of many talents, tough determination, and a tender heart.

The Author

Glen Aubrey is President and CEO of Creative Team Resources Group, Inc. (CTRG), www.ctrg.com. He is an author, business consultant, leadership trainer, conference speaker, professional musician, music writer and orchestrator, and poet.

He has authored *Leadership Is—How to Build Your Legacy, Industrial Strength Solutions Build Successful Work Teams!, Core Teams Work Their Principles and Practices, Growing Core Teams, Core Team Impact!, Go From the Night, Freedom Light, Arranging Notes, L.E.A.D.—Learning, Education, Action, Destiny* and its study guide *Leadership Works,* and *Lincoln, Leadership and Gettysburg.*

You are invited to visit these websites:
www.ctrg.com
www.CreativeTeamPublishing.com
www.Creative-Music-Enterprises.com
www.LeadershipIs.com
www.IndustrialStrengthSolutions.com
www.CoreTeamsWork.com
www.Lincoln-Leadership-Gettysburg.com
www.GoFromTheNight.com
www.Freedom-Light.com
www.Lead52.com
www.glenaubrey.com

The Publisher

Creative Team Publishing (CTP) is a division of Creative Team Resources Group, Inc. (CTRG, www.ctrg.com). CTP was formed in 2007 to publish and distribute business and team development, leadership training, and poetry books, as well as literature of inspiration, insight, human achievement, and positive general interest.

The company's commitment is to make high quality literature available and engage in excellence throughout the process of publication. Customer satisfaction is a top priority. Because CTP practices due diligence in selecting which books it will publish, CTP chooses to work with customers who meet a qualified standard of literary competence and uplifting content.

CTP is a fee-for-service publisher. Products offered include the following:

Pre-Press
1. Editing
2. Proofing
3. Revision
4. Typesetting
5. Four Color Cover Design
6. ISBN
7. Print Set-up

Post-Press
1. Product supply
2. Press releases

Contact Creative Team Publishing. Please visit our company website, www.CreativeTeamPublishing.com, for more information. We look forward to reviewing your literary creation.

Products

Books and curriculum by Glen Aubrey
Available through the Creative Team Publishing Online Store
www.ctrg.com
www.CreativeTeamPublishing.com

Leadership Is— How to Build Your Legacy

Industrial Strength Solutions Build Successful Work Teams!

Core Teams Work Their Principles and Practices

L.E.A.D.—Learning, Education, Action, Destiny
and its accompanying study guide *Leadership Works*

Lincoln, Leadership and Gettysburg

Go From the Night

Freedom Light

Growing Core Teams

Core Team Impact!

Arranging Notes

Music CD Recordings by Glen Aubrey
Available through the Creative Team Publishing Online Store
and Creative Music Enterprises
www.ctrg.com * www.CreativeTeamPublishing.com
www.Creative-Music-Enterprises.com

Beautiful, A Symphonic Experience
Music by Lindamarie Todd and Glen Aubrey

Born Is the King
Christmas Keyboard Reflections
Piano solos

The Custom Album
Piano Solos by Glen Aubrey

Go From the Night Meditation
Glen Aubrey, Solo Piano
Pat Kelley, Guitars
Go From the Night Selected Readings

Meditation
Glen Aubrey, Solo Piano
Pat Kelley, Guitars

Timeless
Glen Aubrey, Solo Piano

Reflecting Hymn
The Rock Album
Piano solos

What Child Is This
Glen Aubrey, Solo Piano

www.ingramcontent.com/pod-product-compliance
Lightning Source LLC
Chambersburg PA
CBHW032336300426
44109CB00041B/1065